UNDERSTANDING BIBLE TEACHING

Revelation

Philip Crowe MA

Scripture Union

47 Marylebone Lane, London W1 6AX

Wm. B. Eerdmans

225 Jefferson Avenue, Grand Rapids, Michigan

ISBN 0 85421 716 9 (Scripture Union)
ISBN 0 8028 1758 0 (Wm. B. Eerdmans)

Printed in Great Britain at the Benham Press
by William Clowes & Sons Limited, Colchester and Beccles

General Introduction

There are many commentaries on the Biblical text and there are many systematic studies of Christian doctrine, but these studies are unique in that they comment on selected passages relating to the major teachings of the Bible. The comments are designed to bring out the doctrinal implications rather than to be a detailed verse by verse exposition, but writers have always attempted to work on the basis of sound exegetical principles. They have also aimed to write with a certain devotional warmth, and to demonstrate the contemporary relevance of the teaching.

These studies were originally designed as a daily Bible reading aid and formed part of Scripture Union's Bible Characters and Doctrines series. They can, of course, still be used in this way but experience has shown that they have a much wider use. They have a continued usefulness as a summary and exposition of Biblical teaching arranged thematically, and will serve as a guide to the major passages relating to a particular doctrine.

Writers have normally based their notes on the RSV text but readers will probably find that most modern versions are equally suitable. Many, too, have found them to be an excellent basis for group Bible study. Here the questions and themes for further study and discussion will prove particularly useful—although many individuals will also find them stimulating and refreshing.

ONE

1 : 'In many ways'

Hebrews 1.1–2.1

At 6.54 B.S.T. on the evening of 17th April, 1970, millions of people around the world paused, anxious, listening intently. After a few minutes' silence, the voice of Jack Swigert was heard. 'O.K. Joe!' Just two words, and the world knew that the crew of Apollo 13 were alive and still in control after a flight which was so nearly a disaster.

'Why is God silent?' people ask. 'Just a few words, and we would know that He is alive and in control.' It is no new question.

> *'And all night long we have not stirred,*
> *And yet God has not said a word!'*

says one of Browning's characters.

The answer to the question is in Heb. 1. 'God has spoken.' He has made Himself known by the things He has said. Man has not discovered God, nor has he come to the conclusion, on the basis of logical deduction, that God exists. The initiative has been taken by God. He has spoken.

The phrase 'in many and various ways' may be translated 'in many degrees and in different ways', but the writer to the Hebrews does not mention the way in which God has shown Himself in creation and in history. He concentrates on the words of God because without His word to guide our understanding, neither creation nor history would have divine meaning for man.

The word spoken 'in these last days' (2) stands in contrast

5

to the word spoken 'of old'; it fulfils and supersedes it. The
revelation of God in Christ is complete (the tense of 'He has
spoken' indicates an action complete in the past), while the
revelation through the prophets was fragmentary. And what
God has done in Christ is for all time, whereas the prophets
spoke 'of old'. The phrase 'in these last days' does not mean
'recently', but 'for this period between the birth of Christ and
the end of this world' (cf. Acts 17.30 f., 2 Pet. 3.1-4). Christ
is the Word of God for *our* age. The risen, living Christ is
God's Word now. In Christ, God has said all there is to say.
The question 'Why is God silent?' is meaningless. The question is—'Will man listen to what God has said and still says
to our age through Jesus Christ?' And for those who have
heard, there is a clear and unusually strong exhortation to
give what might be paraphrased as 'an absolute excess of
attention' to it (2.1).

2 : In Creation

Isaiah 45

The works of God in creation are plain for all men to see.
Anyone and everyone can see the growth of plants and the
life of animals, the sun, the moon and the seas. Yet to the
vast majority of people, the wealth of creation does not inspire
a song of praise like Psa. 103 or 104—'O Lord, how manifold
are thy works! In wisdom hast thou made them all.' Instead,
people believe the sun to be a god or are terrified by unseen
powers in the world which they attempt to placate, or they
abuse the earth's resources in a grasping materialism.

The truth is that God still speaks to men through the creation, but because of sin, men cannot hear. Isa. 45.18 f. links
some of the plainest statements in Scripture about the God
who speaks to the great facts of creation. Three assertions
about creation (18) are paralleled by three statements about
God and His word (18b, 19). The climax is in v. 19b—'I the
Lord speak the truth, I declare what is right.' All this is in
stark contrast to the silence of dumb idols, who even have to
be carried to safety when heathen nations are defeated (20).

There is a similar forthrightness in Paul's statements about
creation in Rom. 1.18-23. What can be known about God is

plain, he argues; 'his invisible nature, namely, his eternal power and deity, has been clearly perceived in the things that have been made' (20).

God's power and deity are also evident in the earlier verses of Isa. **45** which speak of creation (5–12). For man, the creature, to strive with the Almighty Creator is absurd (9). His power is absolute, beyond challenge (11 f.). But that power is also personal. The personal analogies of v. 10 would be grossly inappropriate to the heathen deities and the man-made idols, and the reference to 'my children' in v. 11 implies a personal relationship.

There is an echo, at least, of the word of God in creation, in the experience of a seven-year-old Muslim boy travelling home with his father after his first year at a Christian school. 'There is nothing more beautiful in Yezd,' he wrote later, when he became Bishop in Iran, 'than its sky at night, and its gorgeous mountains in the early morning and in the evening, with the effect of light and shade on them. I remember that, while sitting on the donkey continuing our journey, I started to recite verses about the 8th Psalm: "O Lord, our Lord, how majestic is thy name in all the earth!"'

3 : In Conscience

Romans 2.1–16

In 'The Child's World', Phyllis Hostler discusses modern attempts to 'discard or at least to soften' the idea of conscience. 'But it happens,' she writes, 'that like many other of our grandparents' ideas which we have once discarded, the idea of conscience has returned vigorous as ever. Most of us who have had dealings with little children would assert that if naughtiness is natural, so also are guilt-feelings—that is to say, both arise within the individual without our help.'

Paul's argument in Rom. 2.1–16 is based on two assertions about man's awareness of right and wrong. The first is that everyone has a conscience (15). The same assertion is clearly implied in Rom. 13.5, and in many of the other 32 N.T. passages in which conscience is mentioned (cf. 1 Cor. 8; 1 Tim. 4.2). All men have been created by God with an inbuilt moral radar system, whether they describe it in the vivid words of an African as 'a sharp knife in the belly', or in the terms of medieval theologians as 'the voice of God in the soul'.

The second assertion is explained in relation to the law of God (12 f.). What God said in the law, which 'was added because of transgressions' (Gal. 3.19), He had said previously in creating man with a moral awareness (14, 15a). Paul is as acutely conscious of the effect of the Fall as anyone. His statements about the grim, universal reality of sin are as strong as any written. Yet he can still argue that Gentiles, who have no knowledge of what God has said in the law, can show that 'what the law requires is written on their hearts' (15).

It is thus clear from this passage that in giving all men a moral awareness and a conscience, God has spoken. The Jews may have the law, the oracles of God (3.2), but in the last analysis, Jews and Gentiles are equal before God. He 'shows no partiality' (11). He has spoken to all men.

It must be recognized that it is the gift of conscience itself which may be described, not altogether satisfactorily, as 'the voice of God in the soul'. People may respond to or 'train' their conscience in different ways, but that does not alter the fact that God has given man the capacity to be aware of right and wrong. Conscience is like an alarm-clock—people may switch it off and go back to sleep, but the clock is still there.

For meditation : 'The absolute pitch of the trained musician is akin to the absolute moral pitch of the trained Christian : the wrong note, be it never so little wrong, causes immediate pain' (C. A. Pierce, Conscience in the N.T.).

4 : In History

Genesis 15

For all we know, there may have been many families in the city of Ur of the Chaldeans who decided to pack up all their belongings and move out. Their departure was real and important, both to them and to God. Yet it is Abraham's move which is decisively important for world history, and the reason for this is crucial to our understanding of revela-

8

tion. Abraham's move was based on the command, the promises and the explanations which God gave. All three are in Gen. **15**.

The command is referred to in v. 7 (cf. **12**.1). The promise, first given in **12**.2, which Abraham had begun to doubt as he had got older (8), is renewed in vs. 5 f. and 17–21. The explanation is only hinted at in vs. 12–16 and in the promises; it was not given in full until much later (cf. Rom. **4**). It was the command and the promise of God that mattered more to Abraham (cf. Gen. **22**.1–3, 12, 15–19; Isa. **45**.9).

God speaks in the events of history, which He directs and controls, in the promises which frequently accompany those events, and in the interpretation of the events which He gives. Events on their own may or may not speak to man of God's providence in general terms. It is event and interpretation together which constitute God's revelation of Himself through history.

Gen. **15** does not in fact describe any event at all; the whole chapter is God telling Abraham about past and future events. In view of some modern theories about revelation, it is important to note that Gen. **15** records what God told Abraham about events, and not what Abraham thought about them (1, 7, 13, 18). A widely-held view of revelation is that 'There is no such thing as revealed truth', only 'propositions which express the results of correct thinking concerning revelation' (William Temple). In other words, Scripture contains inspired attempts to understand the divine meaning in events: the phrase 'the word of the Lord came to Abraham' really means, 'Abraham's understanding of what God would have said if He had spoken at all is . . .' Interpreting Scripture then becomes a matter of reconstructing the event and assessing the extent to which the given interpretation of it is true.

Against this view, Scripture claims to be the revealed truth of God. It records what God has done and what He has said about it. The Biblical view is of a personal God, a God who speaks to men.

5 : In Law
Psalm 19

'One of the greatest lyrics in the world', is how C. S. Lewis describes this psalm. Its six verses about nature, five about law and four about man are an anthem of praise to the God who speaks in these three ways. For the psalmist, the connection between the sections is so close and natural that he passes from one to the other without pause or hesitation.

Perowne suggests that the psalmist may perhaps have been gazing at the first flush of an Eastern sunrise. He looks up at the glory of the sky. He watches the sun, and then begins to feel the heat, which develops into 'blinding, tyrannous rays hammering the hills, searching every cranny'. Nothing escapes it (6). 'Then at once, in verse 7, he is talking of something else, which hardly seems to him something else because it is so like the all-piercing, all-detecting sunshine. The law is undefiled, the law gives light, it is clean and everlasting, it is "sweet". No one can improve on this and nothing can more fully admit us to the old Jewish feeling about the law; luminous, severe, disinfectant, exultant' (Lewis).

Each line of vs. 7–9 contains a different noun to denote God's word in the law and a different adjective to describe it, followed by a separate phrase to indicate its effect. The three verses are a marvel of economy in words and rich variety in meaning—the envy of any modern poet! Nor does the symmetry end there. Six times in these verses the psalmist mentions the divine name, and at the final climax of the psalm he brings it up to what was considered to be the perfect number, seven, unobtrusively emphasizing the perfection of divine revelation.

For generations, many Christians have sung this psalm on Christmas Day. Praise to God for His word in creation and in the law prepares them to worship the Word made flesh.

For meditation: Close study of God's words leads the psalmist to pay attention to his own (14).

Questions and themes for study and discussion on Studies 1–5

1. How complete is the knowledge of God which creation and conscience reveal, and how much can man appreciate of that revelation?

2. Is 'the voice of God in the soul' a good description of conscience? (There are not too many N.T. references to look up!)

TWO

The God who Speaks—in Prophets

6 : The Mediums and the Message

Deuteronomy 18.9–22

One of the remarkable features of the Bible is the way in which passages which seem obscure or irrelevant to one generation take on fresh meaning to another. When Matthew Henry wrote Volume I of his famous commentary on the Bible in 1701, he said little about vs. 9–14 of this passage, except to express amazement that even slight remains of such practices could be found in a Christian country. Today, a serial magazine on Myth and Magic is an outstanding commercial success. Ouija boards are sold as toys and used by schoolchildren; and in one week, after a court case in which four teenagers were convicted of desecrating a churchyard for a Black Mass, no less than 28 young people went to a Christian minister for help because they also had been dabbling in witchcraft.

The practices of the pagan nations in Palestine were incomparably worse than this, involving such terrible evils as child sacrifice (10), but though different in degree, they were similar in essence to the black magic and witchcraft practised today. The Bible does not put a hollow 'no' against such practices, leaving a dangerous vacuum (cf. Matt. 12.43–45). The verses which are so clearly and strongly against 'these abominable practices' (12) should never be studied or taught on their own. The whole passage, vs. 9–22, is one unit; v. 15 follows immediately on v. 14. The Lord does not allow sooth-

11

sayers or diviners because He has something far better for the people—His own word spoken clearly by a prophet. The extent to which the initiative in prophecy is taken by God is strongly emphasized. He raises up the prophet (15, 18); He gives the prophet the words to speak (18); and He is responsible for what happens to those who ignore the words of the prophet (19).

Verse 16 can only be understood in relation to Exod. 20. 18 f. and that passage expresses the thoughts of a people deeply conscious of God's holiness and of their own sin. They wanted a prophet as a go-between. Moses himself, while serving in that capacity, looked forward to a better time when all the Lord's people would be prophets (cf. Num. 11.26–30), a time which, in the goodness of God, we now enjoy.

7 : Balaam

Numbers 24

The story of Balaam is one of the most vivid and perplexing illustrations of prophecy that the O.T. contains. He lumbers into the history of Israel astride his renowned talking ass, a heathen diviner one minute and a prophet of God the next. He blesses when he is paid to curse, resolutely holding to God's word. Then he does a complete volte-face, and gives advice which leads to Israel's downfall and his own death, and to him being pilloried in the N.T. as a character of shame.

The parallels between Deut. 18.15–22 and Balaam are significant. Balaam was not one of the children of Israel but a diviner belonging to one of the heathen nations (cf. Deut. 18.14 and Num. 22.7); yet he believed in the Lord God (Num. 22.8) though perhaps also in other gods. In spite of this, God 'raised him up' (Deut. 18.15) to be a prophet on Israel's behalf. Throughout the whole incident, while Balaam swung like a pendulum between God and Balak, God had final control of him. When Balaam eventually spoke, he spoke the words of blessing which God put into his mouth (22.35; 23.12, 16, 26; 24.2 f. 12 f., cf. Deut. 18.18). Even though Balak paraded him from one place to another, hoping that the change of site would change Balaam's message or set him studying heathen omens again (**23**.13–15; **24**.1), Balaam remained steadfast. But the parallel with Deut. **18** does not end with the fact that God chose him and spoke His word through him. Balaam also spoke words God had not commanded him to speak, or perhaps he had reverted to heathen divination (Deut. **18**.20). He suggested that Israel might be seduced into heathen worship at Peor (Num. **31**.16, Rev. **2**.14) and in the war this advice eventually caused, he died (Num. **31**.8, cf. Deut. **18**.20).

Apart from providing an illustration of Deut. **18**, Balaam is an example of a man being used by God without being dedicated to Him. God could and did choose a heathen diviner to be a prophet. He spoke through him. Yet God did not force Balaam into permanent submission, and he remained an erratic, unstable character. We can only conclude that it was by his own choice that he was the sort of character the N.T. holds up to us as a warning.

For meditation : 'I do not want to preach to others, and then to find that I myself have failed to stand the test' (*1 Cor.* **9**.27, *Barclay*).

8 : Micaiah
1 Kings 22.1–28

Being a true prophet was a hazardous, unpredictable calling which might involve death, prison, or glory. Being a false prophet was a different matter altogether. When Jehoshaphat wanted advice, it was a matter of moments to assemble no less than 400 'court' prophets. They were like a diplomatic corps, or like courtiers waiting on a monarch. Their chief concern was to provide impressive arguments to support what their paymasters had apparently decided to do; then as now, people did not want the truth so much as encouragement to pursue the goals they had already set for themselves.

In stark contrast, Micaiah is a vivid illustration of the true prophet of Deut. **18**, and a more 'conventional' one than Balaam. He too was raised up by God. He had the courage to stand against the king, the authorities, and all the massed ranks of false prophets. He had true prophetic conviction, expressed in the classic declaration of vs. 14 and 17–23. And he was content to rest the truth or error of his prophecy on the test set out in Deut. **18**.21 f. (28). What became of him when his prophecy was fulfilled, we do not know.

The contrast between Micaiah and the false prophets recurs repeatedly in the O.T. The true prophets denounced the false ones with great vigour, both for their errors and their greed (cf. Mic. **3**.5, 11; Jer. **14**.14 f.). It is Jeremiah who uses one most striking word to expose the heart of the difference. In Jer. **23**.18, 21 f., he denounces the prophets who scurry around with no message, and says that 'if they had stood in my *council*, then they would have proclaimed my words'. The same Hebrew word for council is used in Psa. **25**.14 ('friendship'); Psa. **55**.14 ('sweet converse'), and Amos **3**.7 ('secret'). It denotes the close, intimate fellowship of God's heavenly council. Then as now, those who declare the true word of God are those who sit in His council, listening to Him.

9 : Prophecy Lost

Amos 7.10–8.12

It is a remarkable fact, just slightly ironical perhaps, that a sermon of an obscure shepherd, which spoke of a famine of hearing the word of God (8.11), should have been preserved for over two and a half thousand years. Amos prophesied sometime in the reign of Jeroboam II (786–746 BC). It was at a time of considerable material prosperity. Amos sees the people as 'idle sprawlers, luxuriating in their choice lamb and veal, improvising their decadent music, pickling themselves in alcohol, and regaling themselves with the finest cosmetics' (Heaton; cf. **6**.1, 4–7). As sometimes happens in times of prosperity, the formal religious life of Israel was flourishing. Not surprisingly, then, there was a sharp clash between the formal, institutional, temple religion and the unconventional, earthy, disturbing, inspired ministry of Amos.

Underlying this exchange between Amaziah, priest of the temple, and Amos, prophet of God, lay the conflict between true and false prophets (10–17). Amaziah imagines that Amos is just another professional prophet who would benefit from learning wisdom and good manners in the provinces before trying to set up in practice in the capital. Amos' reply is

14

revealing. He says that he does not belong to any professional association of prophets. He has not even been trained in the job, but is a herdsman (14, note present tense). Then he said, 'God took me and said, "Go, prophesy." ' It is precisely the same divine calling, the same God-given message, which is the mark of the true prophet from Deut. **18** on.

But the rest of Amos' message appears to run clean contrary to the promises of Deut. **18**. He foresees a time of famine, people searching despairingly for a word from the Lord and not being able to find it (**8**.11 f.). The people had silenced the prophets, ignored them, or scorned them (**2**.11 f.); so God would not let people hear any more. But does this mean that prophecy would cease and revelation come to an end? Surely not entirely. There were no qualifications set against Deut. **18**, and the emphasis in Amos is on a famine of *hearing* the word. Yet whether the prophets were silent, or the people unable to hear, the result would be the same—the people left with no basis for life and no sense of direction. It is tempting—and many have done it—to apply this prophecy of spiritual famine to our own day, which is similar in many ways to life at the time of Amos. But while a good deal of Amos' prophecy is strikingly relevant, **8**.11 f. have to be seen in the light of Joel's foretelling of a new era of prophecy.

10 : Prophecy Regained

Joel 2.21–29

'Are we also among the prophets?' Dr. A. R. Vidler once put that question to present-day Christians, and he commented: 'The fact that the words "prophecy" and "prophet" have not been associated with anything in the living and constant experience of the great churches of Christendom or with normal features of the Christian life does not of course mean that there have in reality been no prophecy and prophets in the successive periods of church history. But I do suggest that the neglect not only of the words, but of explicit recognition of the gifts and endowments which they denote, has been a grave source of loss to the church.' Joel's prophecy was that the Spirit of God would be poured out on all flesh, and sons and daughters would all prophesy (28).

There is no doubt that the first part of this prophecy has been fulfilled. God's Spirit has been poured out. These are the latter days. Every Christian has received the gift of the Spirit. Peter's use of the prophecy of Joel (Acts 2.17-21) and his offer of the gift of the Spirit (Acts 2.38 f.) place that part of the prophecy, and the meaning of the phrase, 'on all flesh' (28), beyond doubt. But what of the gift of prophecy? And what are we to make of the inclusion of 'prophets' in the lists of spiritual gifts (1 Cor. 12.10; Eph. 4.11)?

It may be understood in two ways. One is to recognize that the essence of the prophetic gift is—in Jeremiah's word—a seat in God's council. This intimate fellowship with God, through the Spirit, was once the privilege of a select few. Now it is given to all. The longing Moses expressed has been fulfilled (Num. 11.29). God has poured out His Spirit upon all. There is no longer any need for a go-between to bring God's word to man; all the Lord's people are prophets.

What then of the special gift which is indicated in 1 Cor. 12 and Eph. 4, the gift which Agabus and Philip's four unmarried daughters exercised (Acts 11.28; 21.9-11)? Some maintain that there is evidence of the gift only in the first four centuries of the Christian Church, others that the gift is still exercised today. The central question concerns the nature of the gift. It may be visions and revelations (cf. 2 Cor. 12.1-10); foreseeing future events (Acts 11.28); understanding and expressing Christian truth with unusual clarity (1 Cor. 13.2); or, as J. V. Taylor suggests, 'deliberate involvement in movements for peace, for civil rights, for integration and in action to deal with neighbourhood needs', a suggestion which is in line with the prophetic gift in the O.T.

The gift is not 'recognized' in the Church today in the way Dr. Vidler seems to suggest; would such recognition help? Since all the Lord's people are prophets, it is difficult to believe that God has withdrawn from His Church all four ways in which the special prophetic gift might be exercised.

For meditation : Romans 12.6.

Questions and themes for study and discussion on Studies 6-10

1. How does the test of a true prophet (Deut. 18.22) apply to Christ (Luke 7.16)? Has this test of prophecy any relevance today?

2. Has Acts 2.38, the gift of the Spirit, in any way altered Jer. 23.22, the need to stand in God's council?

3. What is the evidence for and against the continued existence of the gift of prophecy in the Church today?

THREE

The God who Speaks—in Christ

11 : The Word of God
John 1.1–18

The Prologue to John's Gospel is like one of the world's richest diamond mines. Some choice jewels have long been in circulation, brilliantly polished and of incalculable value; fresh discoveries are continually being made; and yet there are still rich resources to be mined.

Most commentaries and study guides find the Prologue so full and suggestive that they take it as several substantial readings, but there is also considerable advantage in deliberately trying to see the picture whole, concentrating on the movement of thought from v. 1 to v. 18. It may be, as many suggest, that various separate strands of thought have been woven into the whole, but there is still a marvellous and significant unity of thought.

The dominant theme is that God speaks. He makes Himself known to man. The opening verses are packed with the key words of revelation—Word, life, light, testimony, witness (1–8); the same is true of the closing verses (14–18). The Prologue as a whole sets out in a chronological framework the full plan of revelation—the historical events and their theological significance. It begins before time, like Gen. 1.1 which it echoes, and it begins with God. 'God's self-disclosure was implicit in the being of God Himself (1). God was never without self-expression' (C. K. Barrett). The world exists, because it is the nature of God to communicate Himself (3);

the life of God is the life and the light of men (4). At v. 5, the stage is set for God's direct intervention. The coming of John is an indispensable witness to the final, complete word of revelation, the appearance of God Himself on the stage of history (6–8), in the life and ministry of Christ. For some at least, this leads to the climax of revelation, new birth by the direct action and will of God (13).

Verse 14 is not the climax of the Prologue; it is a striking repetition of vs. 9–11, and is intended to continue and develop the theme. The word 'beheld' (past tense) refers to the ministry, in which the glory of God was seen; for John, humble, sacrificial love, full of grace and truth, is glory. The witness of the Baptist to the pre-eminence of Christ has been fulfilled (15, which ought not to be in brackets); the continuing evidence of His supremacy is in the grace, the generosity, with which He gives one gift after another to His children (16). John defines grace by contrast with the partial revelation through Moses and the law. In Christ, revelation is complete—it is 'grace and truth' (17). In Christ, God has shown to men everything they need to know. The Prologue began with God revealing Himself to man. It ends with the revelation complete.

For meditation : 'Could anything be more glorious than to have so much to give, and give it all?' (M. Irwin).

12 : God's Word and Christ's Ministry

Luke 4.16–37

The trouble at Nazareth was that they knew Him too well. The reputation of the young Galilean preacher had spread fast (14), and the people of His home town were glad to welcome Him again. Of course, He was invited to preach; and His words, which should have rocked them back on their heels in stupefied silence, aroused only patronizing admiration (22). Jesus had taken a most significant passage of Scripture, Isa. 61.1 f., and had claimed that the things He was doing, of which they had heard reports, were a direct fulfilment of it (21). It was an astonishing claim, but His own people missed it altogether. They were too busy congratulating themselves on having produced such a good local preacher. Then it all turned sour on them. Jesus had stopped short

19

in His quotation from Isaiah; the next words are 'and the day of vengeance of our God' (Isa. **61**.2), which were understood to mean salvation for Israel but vengeance for everyone else. In the rest of His sermon, Jesus shows from the Scriptures that God's favour is no narrow, sectarian privilege to be possessed by one nation; it embraces all (23–27). It was a further explanation of the missionary charter He had taken up in vs. 18 f., with the four main thrusts which characterized His ministry—evangelism, social action, healing and prophecy.

The second congregation, at Capernaum, was astonished at His authority (32) and amazed at His power (36). Their reaction in v. 36 is highly significant if seen in the light of John **1**, not 'Who is this?' but 'What is this word?' They were beginning to realize what the evil spirit had instantly perceived (34, cf. v. 41), that God Himself was speaking directly to men through Christ. To the Jews, the words of ordinary men were more than sounds useful for communication; words had power to achieve results. How much more powerful was God's word! From Gen. **1** onwards (3, 6, 11), the Bible speaks of God's word as a dynamic force · (Isa. **55**.11; Psa. **33**.8 f.). It is this understanding of 'word' which underlines the question the people of Capernaum asked about Christ and it is with the same understanding that we should study such phrases as 'the message (word) of this salvation' (Acts **13**.26), 'the word of life' (Phil. **2**.16), and 'the word of truth' (Eph. **1**.13), all of which stem from God's word in Christ.

13 : God's Word and Christ's Teaching

John 8.21–30

It is really no wonder that the Pharisees were baffled, frustrated, intrigued, and at times furiously angry with Christ. 'Who are you?' they ask, in despairing bewilderment (25). The reply Christ gives is as clear and straightforward as it could possibly be in the circumstances. Had He gone further and claimed to be God, He would have been instantly stoned (cf. John **10**.31–33).

The reply has four main points: Christ has been sent by God (26 f.), His message is from God, with God's full authority (26, 28), what He does and says is always pleasing to God (29), and the most convincing evidence of the truth of this would be given later (28). What Jesus says about the origin of His teaching is, at first sight, parallel to the phrase which occurs so frequently in the O.T. (3,808 times): 'The word of the Lord came to. . . .' But in the O.T., the prophets generally introduced their teaching with the words 'Thus saith the Lord'. Never once does Jesus use this phrase. He spoke as One who had authority. It was His 'Truly I say to you' which astonished the people (Matt. 7.28 f.). The translation 'I do nothing on my own authority' (28), while it emphasizes that Jesus spoke with divine authority, may perhaps be confusing. It is literally 'I do nothing of myself' (cf. 5.30–32). 'If He were to act independently of God (supposing such a thing to be possible) Jesus would be completely powerless. The whole meaning and energy of His work lie in the fact that it is not His work but God's' (C. K. Barrett). His words and His works arise directly out of the deepest possible relationship to the Father, and they therefore reveal the truth of God (26). They are grounded in what William Temple describes as 'this simple claim to divine companionship' (29). On the result of the teaching (30), Temple comments: 'So it always is. When a Christian can say that he has Christ in his heart, and offers a practical obedience as evidence and ground of this, he too wins many for his Lord.'

14 : Christ—the Heart of God's Word
Acts 2.22–39

It is difficult, perhaps impossible, for a Christian of today to imagine himself in Jerusalem, watching and listening as the disciples tumble out on to the streets on the day of Pentecost. The things Peter and the disciples said about the cruelly evil and so recent execution of their Master are so staggering that their first shocking impact can hardly be recaptured. Some oft-quoted words of D. M. Baillie are worth pondering: 'The crucifixion of Jesus set men thinking more than anything else that has ever happened in the life of the human race. And the most remarkable fact in the whole history of religious thought is this: that when the early Christians looked back and pondered on the dreadful thing that had happened, it made them think of the redeeming love of God. Not simply of the love of Jesus, but of the love of God.'

Peter proclaims 'Jesus the Nazarene' as a man whose credentials, 'mighty works, wonders and signs', were clearly divine. His hearers knew this (cf. Luke 7.16; 24.19; John 6.14); they had seen it for themselves. They also knew that He had been executed, and they thought, therefore, that He had died under God's curse (Gal. 3.13). What Peter tells them is, astonishingly, the exact opposite (23). The crucifixion was the will of God. Even though the men who allowed themselves to be responsible for it were 'lawless' evil men, the cross was God's 'definite plan' (cf. 3.18). 'But God raised him' means, from a human point of view, that a tragedy has been turned into a triumph. In terms of God's plan, it means that the revelation is complete and the work of redemption done. The cross alone was half a sentence, a nonsense arousing only despair. The full sentence is clear, true and glorious.

The importance of v. 23, and the depth of meaning in it, may be seen in two other N.T. passages. In Rom. 5.6, Paul talks about Christ's death, and it might be expected that he would go on to speak of this as proof of Christ's love. In fact, he speaks in v. 8 of the death of Christ as the revelation of God's love. The other passage is John 12.32 f. Peter says, in his speech in Acts 2, that Christ is now *exalted* at the right hand of God (33). Exactly the same word is used in John 12.32, 'lifted up', to describe the crucifixion. It means far more than physical movement; it indicates that the cross itself is the glory of God (cf. John 8.28; 13.31 f.). 'The act whereby Jesus is destroyed becomes . . . the final disclosure of the glory of God in the self-giving love which is victorious' (A. M. Ramsey).

15 : 'Seen and Heard'

1 John 1.1–2.6

(This study concentrates on vs. 1–4, and the next on 1.5–2.6)

Like the Prologue to John's Gospel, the first chapter of 1 John summarizes the essential truth about God's revelation. The heart of God's word to man is the 'word of life' (1). He was 'from the beginning', a phrase which, as in John 1.1–3, probably refers to the existence of Christ before time, rather than to the beginning of the ministry; now, that 'eternal life' has been 'made manifest to us' (2). The words emphasize that the revelation is a fact of history, a reality which has been 'heard', 'seen', and 'touched'. 'To have heard was not enough; men heard God's voice in the Old Testament. To have seen was more compelling. But to have handled was the conclusive proof of material reality, that the Word was "made flesh, and dwelt among us" ' (Scott). Revelation is nothing less than God, who existed before all time, making it possible for men to touch Him.

The Greek verb translated 'we have seen' with our eyes' (1) is different from the other verbs—'seen' (1) and 'saw' (2). It 'expresses the calm, intent, continuous contemplation of an object which remains before the spectator. . . . The first two verbs (heard, seen) express the fact, and the second two (looked upon, touched) the definite investigation by the observer' (Westcott).

The rather complicated grammar of vs. 1–3, with v. 2 in brackets and the opening words of v. 3 taking up the theme of v. 1, all leads up to the main verb, 'we proclaim' (3). The central fact of revelation, being a fact of history, must be passed on. In his notable book, 'The Founder of Christianity', C. H. Dodd emphasizes the critical importance of history for Christian faith: 'in these events of ancient time God was at work among men and it is from His action in history rather than from abstract arguments that we learn what God is like, and what are the principles on which He deals with men, now as always. The Church—every gathering of the Church, everywhere, under every form—*remembers* that on a certain night its Founder "suffered under Pontius Pilate". The Church remembers an event which is actual, concrete and in principle dateable like any other historical event'.

For meditation: 'The whole Christian life is a life of remembrance which issues in thanksgiving' (J. Baillie).

16 : 'This is the Message'
1 John 1.5–2.6

It is clear from vs. 1–4 that the heart of the Christian message is the 'word of life' who was seen and heard and intently watched. From the beginning, therefore, handing on the message was an act of memory; those who had seen and heard had to 'testify to it'. But as C. H. Dodd goes on to say, 'It was a memory now illuminated by a discovery that left them at first gasping with astonishment: that the Leader they had thought irretrievably lost had got the better of death itself, in a way as inexplicable as it was indubitable.'

'Memory illuminated'—it is a significant phrase. The message handed on in 1.5–2.6 is far more than basic historical fact; it is the facts plus their meaning. Both together have been 'heard from him' (1.5), that is, from Christ. The life Christ lived showed that God is light (1.5, cf. John 8.12). The death He died was a death which 'cleanses us from all sin' (7, cf. Mark 10.45). Revelation is God alive on earth in Christ, doing things and making it possible for men to understand His action.

The particular way in which the truth is put in 1.5–2.2 is aimed at refuting false teaching. There were heretical teachers asserting either that men were without sin (8), or that men did not sin (10). They maintained that it was possible to have fellowship with God and at the same time to walk in darkness (1.6). Against this, John sets the central importance of God's revelation in Christ (2.1 f.) and the unbreakable link between faith in Christ and obedience to His word (2.3–6). It would be possible to indulge in a theological 'chicken and egg' discourse on vs. 3 and 5; which comes first, assurance and then obedience, obedience and then love, or the other way round. Surely the truth is that a genuine Christian is on an upward spiral; obedience gives greater assurance, and assurance leads to obedience; to keep His word deepens love and deeper love becomes an incentive to obedience. The pattern, both of obedience and love, is Christ Himself (2.6, cf. Phil. 2.8; John 15.12–14).

Questions and themes for study and discussion on Studies 11-16

1. What is the meaning of the description of Jesus as 'the Word of God'?

2. In Christ's ministry, what was the relation between preaching and healing?

3. What is the significance, for our presentation of the gospel, of the N.T. connection between events and their meaning?

24

FOUR

The Jews, the Scriptures and the Messiah

17 : Delight in the Law
Psalm 119.129–144

A few moments' thought about the fuss there is today over laws, rules and authority, followed by another careful reading of Psa. **119**.129–144, makes an astonishing contrast. It would be easy to echo v. 136 and pray for a new spirit of submissiveness. Such phrases as 'thy commandments are my delight' (143) or 'thy law is true' (142) do not exactly capture the spirit of our own age. But we misunderstand altogether what is happening today if we label rebellious students and permissive yippies as 'anti-authority' and imagine we have solved everything. The fundamental problem is not authority and obedience, but reality and stability.

Psa. **119** is a psalm for our day. The psalmist's delight is not in obedient submission to a domineering authority but in the reality and stability of the law. In v. 142, the law is said to be true. It has been 'appointed in righteousness' (138). This means that the commandments of God are true in the sense that they are real, valid, stable. They hold together firmly. They are a solid, reliable foundation for life. And they are so because God Himself is true and righteous. Verse 137 is of crucial importance. The law is righteous because God is righteous. It is just because God is just. The Jews delighted in the law not because it was the authority to which they had to submit but because in the law they touched rock—the reality and eternal stability of God Himself. It was because of that fact that they described the law in terms which may seem to us extravagant.

If the law was 'detached' from the being of God Himself, and given an 'independent' authority, it quickly became either a means of self-righteousness or a crushing burden. For some of the Pharisees, the law was an opportunity for delight in their self-righteousness. In Paul, before his conversion, the law aroused despair. But for those who found in the law the truth of God Himself, it was 'sweeter than honey'.

> Prayer : 'Lord, You are just indeed;
> Your decrees are right.
> You have imposed Your will with justice
> and with absolute truth.
> The justice of Your will is eternal,
> If You teach me, I shall live'
>
> (Gelineau version).

18 : Inspired and Profitable

2 Timothy 3.10–17

Those Jewish children whose parents understood and appreciated the law, and avoided the perils of Pharisaism, were fortunate indeed. Timothy's mother and grandmother were people of sincere faith, which presumably means Christian faith (1.5), but they must have been teaching Timothy the truth of the Scriptures from a time well before their conversion (15, the Greek indicates 'from infancy'). It is of great significance that Paul, a Jewish Christian, gives Timothy strong encouragement to go on studying 'the sacred writings'. They are able 'to instruct you for salvation', in contrast to the corruptions of those 'who will listen to anybody and can never arrive at a knowledge of the truth' (7).

The phrase 'all scripture is inspired' has an alternative translation in the RSV margin, and different translations are grammatically possible. The balance of discussion favours the version in the RSV text, and emphasizes that the whole of Scripture—literally, every single part which goes to make up the whole—is both inspired and profitable.

In using the word 'inspired'—literally, 'breathed out by God'—Paul chose a word which 'accurately expresses the view of the inspiration of the O.T. prevalent among Jews of the first century. The church took it over entire' (J. N. D. Kelly). The word describes vividly the fact of the divine inspiration of Scripture but does not offer any particular theory about how God did it.

Of the four points mentioned to indicate how profitable the Scriptures are, two apparently refer to doctrines and two to conduct. Significantly, two are positive and two negative. There may be some truth in that over-worked modern motto, 'people are right in what they affirm and wrong in what they deny', but it is not the whole truth. If a statement is true, its opposite is untrue. The truth of Scripture is profitable for teaching; the opposite is not. Both teaching and reproof are necessary; correction as well as training in righteousness.

19 : Prophetic Inspiration

2 Peter 1.12–2.3

The Scriptures contain a great many direct statements and other indications of the fact that they are inspired, but the nearest the N.T. comes to a 'theory' of inspiration is in v. 20 f. Like Paul in 2 Timothy, Peter is writing as a Jewish Christian, expressing the understanding of inspiration current among first-century Jews. The 'theory' of inspiration—an indication, that is, of how God did it—is no more than a word in v. 21. Men were 'moved', which means 'carried along', by the Holy Spirit. The word refers to sailing ships. 'The prophets raised their sails, so to speak (they were obedient and receptive) and the Holy Spirit filled them and carried their craft along in the direction He wished' (E. M. B. Green).

This does not mean that the Holy Spirit 'took over' the personalities and mental processes of the prophets and apostles. It implies that He prepared the men, their backgrounds, experiences and circumstances, so that they wrote what God wanted them to write. They were 'holy men', dedicated to God, but also, for the most part, free men. Visions and trances were rare compared to the 'pressure of circum-

27

stances' through which God inspired such writing as Paul's letters.

There are many parallels in history to illustrate this 'process' of inspiration, though none to compare with its results. The plays of Shakespeare, for example, were not written by a man in a trance. According to G. M. Trevelyan, 'His work would never have been produced in any other period than those late Elizabethan and early Jacobean times in which it was his luck to live. He could not have written as he did, if the men and women among whom his days were passed had been other than they were, in habits of thought, life and speech, or if the London theatres in the years just after the Armada had not reached a certain stage of development, ready to his shaping hand.'

Apart from the teaching about inspiration, this passage contains two difficult but important questions of interpretation. In v. 20, the RSV may be misleading in 'one's own interpretation', which makes the verse refer to *our* understanding of Scripture. The Greek means literally 'private unravelling'; it may refer to the inspiration of the prophets themselves, who did not offer their own private views on events, 'because . . .' v. 21 (cf. Phillips).

In v. 19a, two interpretations are possible, neither clear from the RSV. Peter may be saying that the events he witnessed fulfilled and therefore confirmed the truth of prophecy; or that the prophetic word is a more reliable proof of the truth of events than his account. The latter is more consistent with Jewish views of the O.T. 'Since the Jews were in no doubt that everything that the prophets taught came from God, it is no wonder that Peter says that their word is more sure' (Calvin).

20 : Tradition versus Life

Mark 7.1-13

An irate father who wants to 'cut off his son with five new pence' has to *cancel* his will and make another; a Greek father would have had his will *made void*. The same word, used by Christ in v. 13, vividly describes the way in which the Pharisees and Sadducees *cancelled out* God's Word, and set their tradition in its place. Three times in a few verses,

Christ contrasts their traditions with the commandments of God (leave – hold fast, 8; reject – keep, 9; make void – hand on, 13). They talked about 'the tradition of the elders' (5), a phrase which implied an authority and status for tradition similar to that of the law itself; Christ spoke about the traditions of men (7 f.). More emphatic still is the contrast in vs. 10 f., 'Moses said . . . but you say'.

Such distinctions probably horrified the Pharisees. They thought that what Moses said and what they said were one and the same thing, that Scripture and tradition were identical. Over the years, the Jewish Rabbis had built up a formidable body of tradition which codified the law and set out in detail what could or could not be done in almost any situation. Ceremonial hand-washing was a case in point (1–5). Christ says nothing about its value, since it was not commanded in the law but nor was it in conflict with the law. He takes a more potent illustration. Keeping vows was specifically commanded in the law (cf. Num. 30.1 f.); but the Pharisees, in their tradition, spelled out in detail the vows that could be made—such as promising money to God (11). They then realized that some vows might contradict other parts of the law, so they made judgements about priorities, wrong judgements (10–12), and made their tradition more important than God's Word.

How could people who recognized so clearly the authority and full inspiration of Scripture make such blunders? Christ's use in vs. 6 f. of the quotation from Isa. 29.13 indicates that they respected the law but not the Giver of the law. They 'detached' the righteous law from the righteous God who gave it, and inevitably their understanding of it became unrighteous (cf. study of Psa. 119.129–144). They did not serve the just God who gave the law, so inevitably they perverted the just law into injustice.

21 : God's Word or Man's

John 5.30–47

It was inevitable that Jews who exalted their own traditions above the Word of God should miss the central message of the Scriptures. The cause of the injustice which Christ rebuked in Mark **7** is clearly set out in John **5**.39. The word 'search' indicates meticulous scrutiny, close attention to every detail. It suggests the critical approach of a person who will examine a great painting at close quarters to make sure the forms and textures are correct, rather than the admiring gaze of the person who stands back and sees the beauty and colour and design of the whole. The word 'in' is also significant, indicating that they tried to find life in what had been given rather than in the Giver. 'You' in 'you think that in them you have eternal life' is emphatic in the Greek, and Jesus may have had a saying of the Rabbis in mind. Rabbi Hillel used to say, 'He who has gotten to himself words of Torah, has gotten to himself the life of the world to come'.

One inevitable consequence of making the traditions of men more important than the words of God is a greater concern about man's opinion than about God's (44). Whenever men judge or approve of one another on the basis of human tradition, it is an indication that they are doing the very thing they would probably deny most strenuously—rejecting the supremacy and sufficiency of the Scriptures. Writing about youth work on Merseyside, Roger Sainsbury says that 'some people have been shocked at the way some of our young Christians still act; they smoke, they drink, they dance to beat music, they don't have regular times of prayer and Bible study. How can they be Christians? Some might even ask. But often their courage in witnessing in most difficult circumstances has put me to shame.'

Learning to distinguish between Scripture and tradition is difficult but essential. Even to insist on as good, as valuable, a 'tradition' as daily Bible reading, as though it were a divinely ordained practice indispensable to Christian faith, is to stand on the slippery slope which led the Pharisees to reject Christ.

For meditation : 'Traditions which are not in conflict with Scripture are permissible if optional. Traditions which are in conflict with Scripture must be firmly rejected' (J. R. W. Stott).

22 : 'Disobedient and Contrary'
Romans 10.1–21

A chapter which is about the Jews' rejection of their Messiah, and is packed full of O.T. quotations, makes an appropriate

30

conclusion to a group of studies on the Jews, the Scriptures, and tradition.

Paul had himself been 'extremely zealous . . . for the traditions of my fathers' (Gal. 1.14). He knew at first-hand the zeal and the blindness of the Jews. And since he had himself been made righteous by Christ, he has a heartfelt sympathy for those still floundering in the quicksands of human traditions (1, cf. 9.1–3). Rom. 10 is an expansion of 9.30–33. Paul's aim is to show his Christian readers that the way of righteousness is open to everyone (5–13); that the Jews have had opportunity to hear the gospel (14–18); and that they reject it because they are 'disobedient and contrary' (19–21). He does this by stringing together O.T. verses, and interpreting them in a manner similar to that of Jewish commentators, but with this vital difference—that he knew Jesus Christ to be the Messiah.

Verse 5, a quotation from Lev. 18.5, appears to support the Jews' conviction that the law could give life, in contradiction of John 5.39. The verse should be understood both in the light of Luke 10.28, where the first commandment—Love God—is the way to life, and also in the light of Paul's own experience of failure to love God and obey His law. It is significant that he chooses another passage from the law of Moses (Deut. 30.11–14) to illustrate the opposite of v. 5, and to show that righteousness is available to all through faith in Christ. There are important parallels between v. 12 and 3.22 ff. and between v. 13 and Joel 2.32 with Acts 2.21.

In the second part of the chapter, the texts Paul uses answer four points. Everyone must hear the gospel (14 f.), but not all for whom it was intended have accepted it (16 f.). Then have those who rejected it not heard it properly (18), or not understood (19 f.)? It all leads up to a grim warning, particularly for those who believe, as the Jews did, in the full authority and inspiration of Scripture. They were neither ignorant nor stupid, but disobedient and stubborn. In spite of all God gave them, they still missed the heart of the matter.

Questions and themes for study and discussion on Studies 17-22

1. Why, how, and when should false teachers be corrected?

2. What is the value and importance of tradition in the Christian life?

3. Was it true of the Jews, or is it true of Christians, that 'to be the inheritors of a great tradition gives men heroism, and it gives them blindness of heart' (Gore)?

4. How do you reconcile the apparent contradiction between Rom. 3.31 and Rom. 10.4?

FIVE

Christ's use of Scripture

23 : In Temptation
Matthew 4.1–17

In 'The Heart of the Hunter', the explorer Laurens van der Post describes the hard experience of being alone in the vast empty spaces of Central Africa, and its effect on people. 'To be in the wilderness,' he says, 'especially alone, is a fiery test of a man's inner life.' When Christ went through that fiery test, fiercely assailed by Satanic temptations, it was the word of God in the O.T. Scriptures which sustained Him and provided His answers to the temptations.

Christ knew the O.T. so thoroughly that there is great variety in His use of quotations. Sometimes they must be understood in the light of the original context and sometimes not, but it is worthwhile and important to study the context every time. Normally the temptations are understood with reference to Christ's mission as alternative ways of working—a Christian Aid miracle man, a popular wonder worker, or a political compromiser. This interpretation is one of the many probable meanings of the temptations, but it takes little account of the chapters in Deuteronomy from which Christ's answers were drawn. A careful examination of Christ's replies to the temptations, seen in their contexts, may open a deeper level of interpretation. The first answer (4) is from v. 3 in Deut. 8.1–10 which is based on Exod. 16 and 17. The Israelites in the wilderness certainly needed bread but when they were in a tight corner, with supplies running out, would they

33

rely on the word and the command of God, and trust Him, or start a revolt? Christ, facing the same temptation, trusted God's word.

The second answer (7), from Deut. **6**.16, also reflects Exod. **17**. The people were not content with what God chose to do. They wanted proof that He was with them, so they had the nerve to put Him to the test (cf. Mark **8**.11–13). Jesus did not require such proof. What God chose to do was sufficient for Him.

The third answer is from Deut. **6**.13 in the context of vs. 10–15. The people of Israel were to enter a good land, but they would be surrounded by pagans. Would they serve God alone, or compromise? Again Jesus faces a similar temptation. For Him, God alone was more than sufficient.

Seen in the context of the experience of the people of Israel, one part of the meaning of the temptations is relevant to almost every Christian individually and to every Christian community. Few are tempted to perform social or economic miracles, or become the talk of the town by hurling themselves off London's Post Office Tower, trusting in God's care. A great many are tempted to doubt or question the Word of God, the actions of God, and the sufficiency of God.

*For meditation : 'I have laid up thy word in my heart, that I might not sin against thee' (Psa. **119**.11).*

24 : In Teaching

John 10.22–39

Whether He is in acute spiritual danger in the wilderness, or in danger of death by stoning in Jerusalem, it is through the Word of God that Jesus masters the situation. The Jews, despite their devotion to the Scriptures, were getting desperate. Was Jesus the Messiah or not (24)? The answer Jesus gave, which led up to a claim to be equal with God, provided them with an ideal opportunity to solve everything with some well-aimed stones (30 f.).

The quotation of Scripture which Jesus used to persuade them to drop the stones was just five words long and seems obscure to us. To the Jews it was a notoriously difficult verse.

In Psa. **82**.6 it referred to the judges who were charged with administering justice in accordance with God's Word. They were people 'to whom the word of God came' (35) and as such, were called gods (cf. Psa. **82**.1). That being so, Jesus could hardly be guilty of blaspheming for calling Himself 'Son of God' (36).

To the Jews the verse was a problem because it was not easily reconciled with the uncompromising monotheism of the law. Hence Jesus' reminder to them—'scripture cannot be broken' (35). In John's Gospel, 'Scripture' indicates a particular passage; and the word 'broken' means ignored or set aside. The force of the saying is that even so brief and difficult a verse cannot be set aside since it is part of Scripture. It is of great significance that Jesus should make even so brief and controversial an O.T. saying the nub of His argument. The fact that He does so indicates that He shared the Jewish view of the full authority and inspiration of the whole of the O.T.

For further study : 'St. John records the permanent signifi- cance of the O.T. no less than the Synoptists' (Westcott). With John **10**.35, cf. **13**.18; **17**.12; **19**.24, 28, 36.

25 : In Controversy

Matthew 22.23–46

Both the Pharisees and the Sadducees distorted or blunted the truth of God's Word, the former by submerging it in tradition and the latter by superficial interpretation. The question in vs. 24–28 is typically fanciful and legalistic. It is based on a baldly materialistic way of interpreting Scripture, and while it purports to reflect faith in God's Word, it is an expression of unbelief; they do not know the power of God. Christ does not accept their statement, not even as a half- truth. He rejects it as untrue, and refutes their false deduc- tion from Deuteronomy by a proper deduction from Exod. **3**.6. His interpretation is based, not on the surface meaning of the passage, but on the principle behind it.

While the Sadducees are temporarily silenced, the Pharisees seize their chance. Their tradition included hundreds of commandments, and the Palestine Department of Employment must have suffered an appalling loss of productive man-hours while the Pharisees debated the relative importance of them. Verse 36 reflects this debate. Christ's answer, another quotation of Scripture, takes them back to basic principles. Its effect is like a flame-gun going over a patch of dead weeds.

With both the Pharisees and the Sadducees silenced, assuming the latter were still around, Jesus leads them to think again about the Messiah. Once again He uses the Scriptures, a psalm well-known and widely-discussed by the Rabbis. Their 'idol' was a warrior-Messiah, a King like David, whose son he would be. 'But David called him Lord,' Christ points out; 'If David used the divine name to describe the Messiah, how can the Messiah be David's son?' It is such a clear, honest and straightforward understanding of Scripture that it is hardly surprising they stopped questioning. Perhaps they started thinking.

To think over : 'It is by a constant self-criticism of our own idolatries that we Christians can learn again and present to our contemporaries the glory of God in the face of Jesus Christ' (A. M. Ramsey).

26 : Basic Principles

Matthew 5.17–26

Like the foreword to a book, vs. 17–20 set out some basic principles. They explain in advance points which might otherwise be seriously misunderstood. The rest of Matt. 5 must be read in the light of vs. 17–20. It would be easy, and it has often been done, to interpret vs. 21–48 as a new law, contrary to the law of Moses, and aware of this possibility, Christ warns people against thinking that His teaching contradicts the O.T. (17). Verses 18 f. would have been echoed by the Jews of Jesus' time; Josephus, the Jewish historian, writing in the 1st century, says 'We have given practical proof of our reverence for our own Scriptures; for although such long ages have now passed, no one has ventured either to add or to remove or to alter a syllable; and it is an instinct with every Jew, from the day of his birth, to regard them as the decrees of God, to abide by them, and if need be, cheerfully to die for them. Time and again ere now, the sight has been witnessed of prisoners enduring tortures and death in every form in the theatres, rather than utter a single word against the laws and the allied documents.'

It is generally Christian scholars who have over-emphasized what is new in vs. 21–47, taken the teaching of the Rabbis at its worst, and expounded the Sermon on the Mount as a new law. By contrast, the Jewish commentator, Montefiore, concludes that 'Jesus, as the prophetic teacher of inwardness, wanted to show that the true fulfilment of the law included and implied an inward and enlarged interpretation of the leading moral enactments'. When Jesus used the phrase 'You have heard that it was said', followed by an O.T. quotation, it would probably have brought to the minds of His hearers not only the particular law, but also the teaching of the Rabbis on it. He then took the same law, the law He had described in vs. 17–20, and gave an interpretation which, by contrast with current Rabbinic teaching, was 'something finer and deeper, something more inclusive, completing, and profound' (Montefiore).

In Matt. 5 Jesus uncompromisingly endorsed the supreme authority of the O.T., while at the same time penetrating the heart of its meaning.

Questions and themes for study and discussion on Studies 23-26

1. Is it ever right to study a verse of the Bible apart from its context?

2. Study the ways in which Matt. 5.21–48 fulfils rather than contradicts the law.

SIX

The Apostles' use of Scripture

27 : The O.T. in a New Light
Acts 13.16–43

It has been suggested that 'One of the main activities of the Early Church was hunting down prophecies, types and analogies in the Old Testament for the illumination of the mystery of Christ' (S. C. Neill). The suggestion may seem a little far-fetched; surely the Early Church had more important things to occupy them? Were not their main activities worship, evangelism and service? Two weighty factors indicate that Stephen Neill is probably right. The first, already studied, is that the Jews regarded the O.T. as the inspired word of God. Every new happening and every fresh thought had therefore to be either expressly foretold in the O.T. or to be consistent with it. The second, also studied, is that Christ Himself regarded the Scripture as God's word, He frequently appealed to the O.T., and He encouraged His disciples to do the same. The result, further proof of Neill's suggestion, is that at least 10% of the N.T. is made up of O.T. references. One writer has counted 269 direct quotations, and there are several hundred allusions.

It was natural that Paul, speaking in the Jewish synagogues (cf. Acts **13**.15), should appeal frequently to the O.T. The first part of his sermon (16–22) traces the history of Israel through to David. The second part (23–31) follows closely the pattern of Christian preaching which can be clearly seen in other sermons in Acts (cf. **2**.14–39; **3**.13–26; **4**.8–12;

5.30–32; 10.34–43). Part three details scriptural evidence in support of what has been said (32–41). The purpose of these O.T. quotations is aptly stated in vs. 32 f.; Christian preaching is the good news that what God promised to do, He has now done. The first quotation is from a 'Royal Psalm' (Psa. 2.7, cf. Heb. 1.5; 5.5) and it refers to the day when the King of Israel was anointed as the earthly representative of God Himself and adopted as God's son. The two following quotations confirm that the Messiah is greater than David, since He is to receive all the blessings promised to David (Isa. 55.3). The final quotation is particularly fitting as the application of the sermon. Its effect upon the Jewish hearers would have been—'The prophets foretold this day; you have looked forward to it; don't miss it.' No wonder they begged to hear more!

Question: What equivalent can we expect today in evangelism, or in the life of the church, to the 'noble' attitude of the Beroeans (Acts 17.11)?

28 : 'Copies of the true'

Hebrews 8.1–13

The letter to the Hebrews is not one of the favourite letters of the Church today, nor is it generally understood, though it has been described as 'a great and original epistle; the writer had a mind of extraordinary beauty, power and penetration' (S. C. Neill). The reason it is difficult for us to understand is simply that, for the most part, we are not Hebrews. The letter was addressed to Jewish Christians for whom the O.T. was the whole Bible, but 'the interpretation was new; everything was now understood Christologically, and the Old Testament was ransacked to discover the categories in which the reality of Jesus the Christ could be expressed, and to work out the parallels between the mighty acts of God on behalf of His people of old and those new and even mightier acts in which the Christian people felt themselves to be involved' (Neill).

The use made of the O.T. ranges from simple illustration (1 Cor. 9.9 from Deut. 25.4) to the more elaborate 'types' in Hebrews. In Heb. 8.1, the writer begins a summary of the argument of earlier chapters. He points out to his Jewish readers, whose religious life before their conversion had centred on the covenant, the temple, the priesthood and the sacrifices, that Christians have the true reality of all these. The originals were 'copies' and 'shadows'. The 'tent' Moses erected was made according to the 'pattern' (Gk. type) he was shown (5). Between the original type and the final reality there is a direct historical correspondence which guides our understanding. Christ is the true High Priest (1), serving in the real (true) sanctuary (2); He has offered the pure sacrifice (cf. NEB margin, 'have had something to offer', 3; see 7.27; 9.14); He mediates the better covenant (6). He has given the final and true reality to the original types. Significantly, the writer gives a long, direct O.T. quotation to confirm this interpretation (8–12, Jer. 31.31–34). Types and quotations together emphasize the fact that the O.T. and N.T. are essentially one, to be understood together. Our difficulty with Hebrews is that we are not sufficiently familiar with the O.T. book with which it corresponds, the book of Leviticus.

29 : 'Now this is an allegory'

Galatians 4.21–31

It was C. H. Spurgeon who first popularized the story of the famous tailor whose final word of advice to the 'knights of the thimble' gathered round his death-bed was 'Always put a knot in your thread'. In the same lecture, Spurgeon spoke of illustrations as 'burrs sure to cling to our clothes' when out walking; 'brush as we may, some relics of the fields remain upon our garments; so there ought to be some burr in every sermon that will stick to those who hear it'. Paul's allegory of Hagar and Sarah is just such an illustration. He has argued in many ways in Gal. 1–4 for freedom through Christ and the gospel, as against slavery under the law. This allegory is the knot in the thread. Unlike a type, it does not depend on the original meaning or significance of the O.T. story. It is simply an illustration, and the truth of it depends on other teaching. It is the knot which cannot exist without the thread of truth already set out.

If interpreting the O.T. in this way seems strange to us, it must be remembered that Paul was speaking directly to those 'who desire to be under law' (21). They had four ways of interpreting the O.T., the literal, the suggested, the logical, and the allegorical. Paul, a proficient, well-trained Rabbi, was meeting the legalists on their own ground and offering them what they considered to be the most elevated method of interpretation to confirm his point. By contrast with the elaborate, rambling allegories of the Jews, the Greeks and some later Christians, Paul's use of allegory is remarkably restrained. He uses it only for those familiar with the method, to illustrate rather than to provide a basis for truth.

Question : Can you summarize in one sentence the central point of Paul's allegory, in the light of which the detail should be understood? Cf. 3.1–14; 4.1–7.

30 : The Moving Rock
1 Corinthians 10.1–13

The three previous studies which have been concerned with the apostles' use of Scripture have been based on passages addressed to Jews. For them, the O.T. was full of meaning, as it was also for the 'god-fearers', many of whom became Christians. But what of the Gentiles? What use did the apostles make of the O.T. when addressing a mixed church of Jews and Gentiles, such as the church in Corinth? There are several hints in the language of 1 Cor. 10, quite apart from the substantial use Paul makes of O.T. history. He refers to 'our fathers' (1), 'warnings for us' (6), and 'our instruction, upon whom the end of the ages has come' (11). There is some evidence that Paul was slightly more restrained in using the O.T. with Gentiles, but not much. In Acts 17.22–31, for example, when speaking at Athens, Paul did not quote the O.T. directly, but he alluded to it. In his letters to Gentiles, his teaching is full of the O.T.

In 1 Cor. 10, he uses some events in the history of Israel to provide important lessons for Christians. The Israelites had great privileges, he points out, but still they failed to please God (1–5); and he then spells out and applies the reasons for their failure, concluding with a warning (12) and with encouragement (13). There was a recent example of the value for Christians of such O.T. teaching when the Anglican Church

Missionary Society moved its British headquarters in 1966. The General Secretary, Dr. J. V. Taylor, wrote shortly before the move: 'In recent months my mind has often returned to that very strange reference in the first Epistle to the Corinthians to that supernatural rock which accompanied the travels of the People of God. I presume that St. Paul was taking as his parable the legend which the rabbis passed on that the Rephidim rock from which the waters had gushed forth to quench the thirst of Israel followed them about in all their subsequent wanderings. The idea of the marching rock is not, after all, so weird to anyone who has motored across the plains of South India or Eastern Uganda and seen how one isolated crag seems to stay with the traveller hour after hour. This is an apt and evocative image of that which is permanent and reliable in the midst of change, an image of Christ Himself, but also of the unchanging call of Christ and of that identity which obedience to the call gives to us. The rock symbolizes both the changeless "I am", and also the changeless "Thou art" which God addresses to us. I have always felt it to be significant that when Moses in Midian was confronted with the awful adventure to which God was sending him, his first two questions were: "Who am I?" and in so many words, "Who are you?". Without a sense of identity, without an assurance of what we are meant to be, we become paralyzed and totally unable to go forward into the unknown. And this is a very common malaise of these days.'

Note: While it is possible that Paul had the rabbinic legend in mind, he may well have been speaking metaphorically, 'i.e. wherever the Israelites were, the supply never failed' (IVP, NBC). This does not lessen the relevance of Dr. Taylor's words, but serves to high-light an aspect of the apostle's use of Scripture.

31 : 'For our instruction'
Romans 15.1–13

Again in this passage, as in 1 Cor. 10, Paul tells both Jews and Gentiles alike that the Scriptures were written for *our* instruction (4). In 15.1 f., he is completing the argument he has been working out in ch. **14**. The climax of his teaching is the example of Christ, who 'did not please himself' (3). It is extremely unlikely that any preacher or teacher today would want to add anything to that climax, but Paul does. Those three words which occur so often in the O.T.—'It is written' —introduce a quotation which has something to add even to teaching based on Christ's example. Psa. **69** is frequently used in the N.T. (cf. John **15**.25; **19**.28–30; Rom. **15**.3) and the other half of the verse quoted in Rom. **15**.3 appears in John **2**.17. Paul uses the psalm to describe Christ as 'being so identified with the cause of God that He endures in His own person the assaults of the enemies of God' (Dodd). Significantly the quotation refers to Christ's faithfulness to God and its use to confirm the exhortation in v. 2, 'let each of us please his neighbour', implies a close link between obedience to God and consideration for others. In vs. 9–12, Paul again strings together several O.T. quotes to reaffirm the point made often in Romans, that Christ is the servant of Jews and Gentiles alike.

The way he uses these passages of the O.T. is an object lesson in the truth of vs. 4 f. The purpose is hope, the means is steadfastness (cf. 2 Cor. **6**.4, 'great endurance'; Heb. **3**.14), and the encouragement of the Scriptures. The value of the O.T. for us has been quaintly but aptly expressed by Bishop Moule: 'Not only is it, in its Author's intention, full of Christ; in the same intention it is full of Christ for us. Confidently we may explore its pages, looking in them first for Christ, then for ourselves, in our need of peace, and strength, and hope.'

Questions and themes for study and discussion on Studies 27-31

1. What similarities are there between Heb. **9**.11–14 and Lev. **16**.1–14?

2. What lessons are to be learnt from 1 Cor. **10** about the way in which 2 Tim. **3**.15 f. should be put into practice?

SEVEN

Principles and Problems

32 : Supreme Authority
John 17.1–19

The key words at the beginning and end of this passage, authority (2, Phillips) and truth (17), sound strange among the discordant noises of popular thought. Today's theme words are tolerance and synthesis; 'the open mind has become a yawning chasm,' writes Richard Hoggart, and 'truth' lies in a futile piecing together of the ideas of men.

The word translated authority or power (2) 'is a very comprehensive term and excellently suited to express the idea of an all-inclusive authority, in the sense of the freedom and the power to command and to enforce obedience, and to have possession of and rule and dominion over' (Geldenhuys). It is used in Matt. 21.23 where the chief priests ask Jesus 'By what authority are you doing these things, and who gave you this authority?' The answer, which they were not given at the time because they were not able to receive it, is that Christ was given authority from God the Father, authority 'over all flesh, to give eternal life' (2).

Yet though He has power to enforce obedience, Christ does not do so. He is not an authoritarian figure, compelling obedience and enforcing submission without regard for individual freedom. Christ's authority is to *give* eternal life, not to force it on people. 'As a redeeming authority, it says "Be free and obey." It does not say, "Obey and be free." ' (Forsyth). This is precisely the sort of authority which people need and which

44

many today are feeling after. It is against authoritarian rule, whether in politics, university or Church, that people rebel.

Christ expressed this redeeming authority by giving to the disciples the words of God (8, 14). He claimed that His words were the words of the living God, and that He spoke not with human authority, but with the authority of God Himself (cf. 12.49). It is all summed up in v. 17, 'thy word is truth'. All the words of God form a single, sufficient, coherent whole, which is not merely true, but truth.

For meditation: Consider the four consequences which flow from the words of Christ—faith (7 f.); joy (13); opposition (14); dedication (18 f.).

33 : 'Even so I send you'

Galatians 1.1–2.2

The roots of the authority of the apostles are indicated in John 17.8. They had been given the words of Christ, they had received them, and they believed and knew the truth. They knew that Christ was Himself *the* Apostle (Heb. 3.1), sent from God. When the Risen Christ showed Himself to them and commissioned them (John 20.19–23), they in turn became Christ's apostles. Their authority was accepted in the Early Church, and to the question—'What happened to their authority when the apostles died?'—the answer is that apostolic authority remains where it always was, in the apostolic word. The Scriptures contain both the apostolic witness to Christ and their instructions for the life of the Church, which the early Christians received as the words of Christ Himself (1 Thess. 2.13; 2 Pet. 3.2).

The dispute in some churches was over the authority of Paul (cf. 1 Cor. 9.1 f; 2 Cor. 12.11–13; 1 Tim. 2.7). The basis of the uncompromising apostolic authority which he exercised was his experience on the Damascus Road, and it is that experience which underlies this passage in Galatians. Paul almost certainly knew the facts of the gospel before he set out for Damascus (13). He had listened to Stephen and probably to other Christians. What he needed to know was the truth and the meaning of those facts, and that is what Christ gave him in a blinding moment of revelation (12). When he saw

45

and heard the risen Christ, Paul knew that reports of the resurrection were true. God had raised Him. The curse of death on a tree had been transformed into a blessing (3.13 f.).

This revelation did not itself make Paul into an apostle. A comparable, if less dramatic, vision of Christ has not infrequently been a feature of the conversion of Muslims. Paul not only saw Christ, thus becoming a witness to the resurrection, but he was also specifically commissioned by Christ to be an apostle to the Gentiles (16). Paul's apostleship is therefore set on precisely the same basis as that of the other apostles.

In 1.18–2.2, Paul emphasizes that his knowledge is independent of, but consistent with, that of the other apostles. He knew the truth direct from Christ. He was an apostle by the direct action of Christ (1). But he was also humble enough, and wise enough, to make sure that his gospel was the same as that preached by the other apostles. Like them, Paul could and did claim that he spoke with divine authority (2 Cor. 13.10; 1 John. 1.5).

For meditation : 1 Thess. 2.13.

34 : 'As originally given'
1 John 5.1–12

It is one thing to recognize that the original words of the Scriptures have divine authority. Whether the text of the Bible as we have it is precisely the same as the original words of Scripture is another question altogether. The phrase which appears in some doctrinal statements concerning the authority of the Bible, 'as originally given', is a straightforward recognition of the fact that some error has crept in as the text has been passed on. How, and how much?

The two passages chosen to illustrate this problem are both worth studying as a whole for what they say about God's Word, but the particular textual point of interest in 1 John 5 is in vs. 7 f. The AV is significantly different from later versions. It includes the words 'there are three that bear record in heaven, the Father, the Word and the Holy Ghost: and these three are one'. And after the words in v. 8, 'There are three witnesses', it adds 'in earth'. John Stott describes the whole of this addition as a gloss, and he points out that 'the words do not occur in any Greek manuscript, versions or quotation before the fifteenth century' (Tyndale Commentary, p. 180).

What may have happened is that a studious monk added what he thought was a helpful note in the margin of his copy of 1 John, and the scribe who copied the manuscript later included the note in the text. Great care was taken in copying manuscripts, but mistakes were sometimes made—such as the inversion of letters, 'scared' for 'sacred'; the omission of a word, such as 'not' in the commandment concerning adultery in the 'wicked' Bible; the addition of words, such as 'and fasting' in Mark 9.29; or the substitution of what is familiar for what is unfamiliar.

The RSV and most other recent translations do not even include the extra words of 1 John 5.7 f. in the margin, as these translations are based on more complete and more accurate manuscript evidence. The verses, though still difficult, are easier to understand without the monk's tidy gloss, which Stott describes as 'not a very happy one'. 'The threefold testimony of verse 8 is to Christ; and the Biblical teaching about testimony is not that Father, Son and Holy Spirit bear witness together to the Son, but that the Father bears witness to the Son through the Spirit.'

For study: Does the comment on v. 8 apply also to the witness to the truth of God's Word? (cf. John 16.12–15).

35 : A Thousandth Part
Revelation 1

The hymn 'With harps and with viols', which is always sung with such gusto by Welsh choirs, has a chorus based on Rev. 1.5—'Unto Him who hath loved us and washed us from sin . . .' The word 'washed' appears in the AV; in the RSV, it is 'freed'. The difference of a word in English is only a letter in Greek, *lusanti*—freed, or *lousanti*—washed. It makes a significant though not a vitally important difference to the meaning.

The word 'freed' is more generally accepted as being the original, not because it appears in more manuscripts, but because it appears in those that are most reliable. Students of the text have to try to trace the pedigree and assess the value of the different manuscripts; they cannot solve all problems simply by counting the number of times different readings appear and accepting the one which appears most often, since any number of manuscripts may copy one wrong one. In his biography of Asquith, Roy Jenkins describes the break-up of relations between Asquith and Lloyd George in 1916. His main source is Beaverbrook's 'Politicians and the War'. There are other books on the subject, but as Jenkins points out: 'almost all lean heavily, with or without attribution, upon Lord Beaverbrook's version. . . . It is therefore often the case that, at first sight, a statement appears to be overwhelmingly confirmed from about six different sources; but on closer examination, the six sources all turn out to be subsidiaries of the central Beaverbrook fount.'

The impression could easily be gained that the whole text of Scripture is in the melting pot. Nothing could be further from the truth. The famous Cambridge Greek scholar, Hort, estimated that differences in the text made up no more than a thousandth part. No major doctrine is disputed because of doubt about the text. By comparison with documents of similar age, it is remarkably well-preserved.

This is no more than we should expect. There would be little point in the Spirit telling John to 'Write what you see in a book and send it to the seven churches' (11) if the Spirit did not intend ensuring that it would reach not only the seven churches but ourselves as well, for whom it was also intended.

For further study : As with 1 John 5, the passage chosen to illustrate one textual point has a great deal else to say about God's Word; see especially vs. 1–3 (cf. 22.16–19).

(Other aspects of Rev. 1 will be the subject of a later study.)

36 : History, Legend or Myth

Genesis 3.1–21

Any great complex of literature brings together many different literary forms—historical narrative, poetry, legend, myth, letters, parables—and it is of great importance that each form should be interpreted on its own terms. Parables should not be treated as historical fact; legend should be understood as an interpretation of and witness to the truth of history; while a myth may be treated as having no connexion with history at all. 'The word myth is used of those majestic tales, such as the early stories in Genesis, in which a profoundly religious understanding of the human situation, such as can hardly be better conveyed than through such a tale, is made known to us' (S. Neill). On that understanding, Genesis 1–3 may be understood without any reference to history at all.

This approach is only possible if the way in which the N.T. interprets Genesis is ignored. From Gen. 1 and 2, the N.T. teaches that the human race is 'from one' (Acts 17.26); and the offence is of one man (Rom. 5.12–19) who is 'as distinct an individual as were Moses and Christ. These guidelines exclude the idea of myth and assure us that we are reading of actual, pivotal events' (D. Kidner, Tyndale O.T. Commentaries). Similarly, with regard to Gen. 3, the N.T. assumes and argues from the historical reality of the Fall (cf. Luke 3.23 ff.; Rom. 5.18 f.; 1 Cor. 15.20 f.).

If Gen. 3 is not myth, what sort of history is it? Kidner suggests a possible answer in a parallel between Gen. 3 and two chapters in 2 Samuel. In 2 Sam. 11, which is historical fact, an account is given of David's sin against Uriah. 2 Sam. 12.1–6 puts that same history into legend form in order to interpret it. The question is—is Gen. 3 equivalent to 2 Sam. 11 or 2 Sam. 12.1–6?

37 : Contrasts
Matthew 28.1–8; Luke 24.1–11

The narratives of the resurrection pose in an acute form the problem of disagreements in Scripture. The accounts attest vividly the central fact, but there are several differences of detail. A careful comparison of all four accounts reveals that different groups of women come; they come at different times; details about the stone and descriptions of the messengers are not the same; and in Luke 24 and John 20, Jesus appears in Jerusalem, while in Mark 16 and John 21 He appears in Galilee.

There are two ways of approaching this sort of problem. The first is to attempt to harmonize the facts and make all four accounts into a single coherent record. Geoffrey King's

'The Forty Days' is a good example. This approach is valid up to a point, as major discrepancies, sufficient to cast doubt on the credibility of the record, could not be tolerated. Even so, attempts to harmonize every detail of the resurrection accounts are generally remarkable more for their ingenuity than for the conviction they carry. The historical reliability of the Bible does not depend on the successful harmonization of every detail of differing accounts.

The second approach is to understand the documents and explain the origin and significance of the differences. The Gospels do not record the findings of a Royal Commission appointed to inquire into an extraordinary event. They tell us how the fact was first realized. In the Early Church, the fact of the resurrection would be told, together with a detailed description of what happened, to one or two witnesses. Gradually, the main centres of Christian life—Jerusalem, Caesarea, Rome, Ephesus—would accumulate their own accounts, preference being given to the narratives connected in any way with local people. The four evangelists, when they came to write, recorded faithfully the accounts given at the centres with which they were associated. Each writer gives an incomplete account; probably all four accounts together do not include all the details.

Such differences as these confirm rather than deny the central fact. Exact correspondence in every detail arouses suspicion rather than belief. In a famous tribunal of inquiry concerned with methods of police interrogation, one member of the tribunal said, in giving judgement against the police, 'The mechanical precision with which the chief police witnesses corroborated every detail of each other's statements cast suspicion upon their evidence.' No such suspicion attaches to the accounts of the resurrection.

38 : Self-Consistent

Matthew 25.31–46

Again and again in Christian history, and especially in recent theological writing, these verses have been interpreted in a way which suggests that they contain the whole of Christian faith. A Jewish writer, C. G. Montefiore, says of vs. 33–40, 'The charity rendered, the loving service paid . . . is regarded by

Christ as if rendered to Himself. There need not even be the conscious thought that it is done for Christ or in His name. This is splendid doctrine. The loving deed is enough. No purer account, no more exquisite delineation of Christian philanthropy was ever penned. It is broad, liberal and truly religious.' On the face of it, these verses set OXFAM supporters, 'Shelter' helpers, and prison visitors, Christians and non-Christians, on the same basis—that of judgement by works and not by faith.

The two principles of interpretation which must be remembered in studying a passage like this are the self-consistency of Scripture as a whole and the importance and value of each section. God's word is truth—one part of Scripture does not contradict another; and 'every inspired scripture is profitable', including the genealogies.

The total understanding of Scripture, within which the interpretation of Matt. 25 must be set, is that the N.T. teaches two truths with equal emphasis. First, we are made acceptable to God only by Christ—'it is God who puts us right' (Rom. 8.33)—and not by anything we do. Secondly, it is by what we do that we are recognized as God's. Both these truths are clearly taught by Christ and by the apostles. Both are evident in the Gospels and in the writings of Paul and James. A passage like Matt. 25 or Jas. 2, which concentrates on the second truth, must be set alongside the first, without being either ignored, diluted, or misinterpreted.

It is possible that in all the discussion about reconciling Matt. 25 with Christian theology as a whole, the heart of the passage is missed. It 'should be understood as Jesus' farewell speech to His disciples. The accent falls not so much on the surprise (37–39), or the unconscious goodness or badness; that is only a rhetorical device which gives further weight to the sentences repeated in vs. 40 and 45. Thereby Jesus, at His departure, makes the rank-and-file brother in need His representative; He identifies Himself with him' (K. Stendahl).

Questions and themes for study and discussion on Studies 32-38

1. What is the relation between the teaching of Jesus as recorded in the Gospels and God's authority today?
2. How and to what extent was Jesus influenced by the times in which He lived, and what effect does this have on the authority of His teaching?

EIGHT

Understanding Scripture

39 : Understanding O.T. History
Exodus 15.22–27

Countless sermons on the cross have been preached from this straightforward historical narrative, with v. 25 as the focal point. 'Some', says Matthew Henry, 'make this tree typical of the cross of Christ, which sweetens the bitter waters of affliction.' Another commentator makes no mention of the historical situation in Exodus, or of the meaning of the event for Israel, but concentrates exclusively on a figurative interpretation: 'The tree is the picture of the cross . . . the cross was cast, as it were, by God into the bitter waters of the world . . . it was the means of making the bitter waters sweet and turning death into life for all who believe.' Is this interpretation legitimate?

Two guidelines for interpreting O.T. history can be illustrated from this passage. The first is that the narrative must be studied in its original setting; what were the circumstances and what did the event mean for those involved at the time? The people were desperate for lack of water—three days of sand and sun were more than enough (22); and when they found water, it was unfit to drink. The people murmured, Moses prayed, and God 'showed him a tree', one which may have had special natural properties with which some Arabs today are familiar. The primary and central lesson is that God is to be trusted, 'acknowledged not only in the creating of things useful for man, but in discovering their usefulness'

(Matthew Henry). Many other direct lessons could also be drawn from the passage, all from historical understanding of the original meaning.

The second guideline is that figurative or allegorical interpretations of historical narrative are possible if they are consistent with scriptural truth as a whole. Christ's use of the brazen serpent and Paul's allegory of Hagar and Sarah are examples (John 3.14–15; Gal. 4.21–31). The difficulty with this sort of interpretation is that it can lead to all sorts of wild and fanciful ideas, and a useful rule is suggested by A. M. Stibbs: 'Such practice needs to be employed only with great restraint and wherever possible, with confirming scriptural justification. Otherwise it gives unlimited scope to arbitrary fancy, and opens the door for men to read into Scripture almost anything they wish to see there.'

Question: Is there sufficient 'scriptural justification' for interpreting the tree as the Cross?

40 : Understanding N.T. History

Mark 4.35–41

The principles which apply to the interpretation of O.T. history apply equally to the N.T. Like Exod. 15, Mark 4 has been given both strictly historical and marvellously fanciful interpretations. The three questions to ask about a particular passage of N.T. history are what is its significance in the particular setting (is there some word of explanation from Jesus, or a reaction from the crowd)? What is its meaning in the total ministry of Jesus, or in the life of the Early Church? And what is its bearing on life today?

In Mark 4, there is both an explanation and a reaction (40 f.). 'What is the matter?' Jesus asks. 'Don't you know who I am? Don't you trust me?' 'Who is this?' the disciples wonder, awestruck. 'Even wind and sea obey him.' The primary meaning is clear; Jesus is Lord of Creation. He is able to control nature. To the disciples, such power could mean only one thing—Jesus must be God. But at that early stage in His ministry, such a conclusion was too much for them; the event was one among the many evidences which led them eventually to acknowledge Jesus as God's Messiah. The passage has the same primary and central meaning for us today; it is one part of the evidence for believing in the deity of Jesus. The original historical meaning is still significant today.

There have been plenty of figurative and allegorical interpretations of the passage. The most common is that of Tertullian: 'that little ship represented a figure of the Church, in that she is disquieted in the sea, that is, in the world, by the waves, that is by persecutions and temptations, the Lord patiently sleeping, as it were, until roused at last by the prayers of the saints, He checks the world and restores tranquillity to His own.'

Question: more difficult than on Exod. 15! Is there scriptural justification for Tertullian's interpretation?

41 : Understanding O.T. Prophecy

Amos 9.11–15

Men of equal conviction about the inspiration and authority of the Bible, of equal ability in their understanding of language and meaning, and of equal devotion to Christ, have come to different conclusions about the interpretation of prophetic scriptures. That fact underlines the need for careful study, humility, and restraint.

It is important to recognize that prophets spoke about past, present and future events. It is necessary therefore, as with historical narrative, to understand the prophecy in its original setting and to study its meaning for the people to whom the prophet spoke. The last words of Amos' prophecy would have given the Jews a glimmer of hope to gaze at while the grim events of the rest of his prophecy took place. Verses 11–15 would have been appreciated by them as 'a very pleasant piece of music, as if the birds had come out after the thunderstorm and the wet hills were glistening in the sunshine' (Adam Smith).

After studying the verses in their original historical context, the possibility of later fulfilment in Christ or of direct application to our own times should be examined. The prophets

54

spoke for their time and for the future, but often without any awareness of possible fulfilment centuries later (cf. 1 Pet. **1.**10–12). Amos **9.**11 was quoted by James at a critical moment in the life of the Early Church as the pivot of his judgement about the admission of Gentiles to the Church (Acts **15.**16–18). There is no doubt about the scriptural justification for this interpretation!

42 : Parables

Luke 16.1–13

No less than one third of Jesus' recorded teaching consists of parables—about 60 of them in all. C. H. Dodd gives an instructive definition : 'A metaphor or simile, drawn from nature or common life, arresting the hearer by its vividness or strangeness and leaving the mind in sufficient doubt about its precise application to tease it into active thought.' That last part fits precisely the experience of the disciples; 'Now you are speaking plainly, not in any figure!' they said in relief on one occasion (John **16.**29). They would have totally rejected any attempt to explain the parables as simple moral tales.

Some principles of understanding parables stand out from the story of the dishonest steward. The first is that parables are not allegories. Some, like the sower, or the wheat and the tares, may allow for the interpretation of every detail, but most teach one main lesson. If the dishonest steward is treated as an allegory, the result is hopeless doctrinal confusion.

The second principle is that we must study parables in their historical context. Some knowledge of first-century business methods is essential to a full understanding of the dishonest steward (which emphasizes, incidentally, that we do not honour Christ by simply telling without explanation the parable of the lost sheep to Merseyside children who know nothing about sheep or shepherds).

The key to the interpretation of the dishonest steward is v.8. The steward pulled a fast one on his master. He was dishonest; what he did was sharp practice. He is commended for 'prudence' (8), for shrewdness. He is not himself a pattern for Christians, nor is his dishonesty, but his shrewd use of money is. Verse 9 sums up the lesson for us: 'Show that you are Christians by using money. Don't bury it—use it to serve people. And when money no longer counts for anything, the people you have served with it will be waiting to welcome you into eternal life.'

As is often the case with a parable, the verses which follow (10–13) do not interpret or explain it; they expand and develop it. To interpret a parable in the light of succeeding verses can be misleading.

43 : Paul's Letters
2 Peter 3.8–18

It should not surprise us that the quick, volatile mind of Paul, and his mercurial personality are so clearly apparent in his letters. We have already noted that God uses rather than 'takes over' personality.

Peter was by no means the last Christian to utter a perhaps slightly regretful warning on Paul's letters (15 f.). Dr. H. Chadwick mentions a number of theologians who 'were not always certain that they understood him and even, at times, wished that the apostle had sometimes expressed himself with more caution and finesse'. He quotes a most significant and instructive comment from one Methodius in the third century: 'You should not be upset by the sudden shifts in Paul's arguments, which give the impression that he is confusing the issue or dragging in irrelevant material or merely wool-gathering. . . . In all his transitions he never introduces anything that would be irrelevant to his teaching; but gathering up all his ideas into a wonderfully harmonious pattern, he makes all bear on the single point which he has in view.'

The 'ignorant and unstable' twisted Paul's letters by taking one part and ignoring others. They concentrated on 'free grace' and wallowed in total permissiveness, forgetting the clear moral implications of the gospel (cf. Rom. 6); or they missed the central issue and lapsed into bondage (cf. Gal. 1.6). But while every Christian may find Paul's letters hard to understand, it is only the 'ignorant and unstable' who 'twist' them to 'their own destruction'. Ignorance and instability are to be countered by a continual growth in knowledge and grace (18).

44 : Visions and Symbols

Revelation 1

One of the greatest living preachers, Helmut Thielicke, says of Revelation, 'The last book of the Bible remained obscure and dark for centuries, and now all of a sudden, amidst the catastrophes of our time, it is as if the dark wraps had been removed from this book and the broad landscape of history is plain and in it the wonderful highways of God, all of which by roundabout ways lead to the distant, blue hills from which cometh our help.' That may be so, but Revelation remains one of the hardest books in the Bible to understand.

It is usually described as apocalyptic, the Greek word for revelation, meaning literally to unveil something previously hidden. Vivid word-pictures and symbols are used to represent truths, some of which could not be openly stated for political reasons (cf. parts of Daniel and Ezekiel, e.g. Dan. 7). The meaning may be for either the present, or the future, or both. Rev. 1.1 indicates that the book had an immediate relevance to first-century Christians; the word 'soon' must be given its due weight (cf. vs. 3, 19 and 22.10). This means that, as with history and prophecy, the first step in understanding is to examine the actual situation to which the book spoke.

On this basis, remembering the harsh persecution of the Church by the imperial power towards the end of the 1st century, we look for truth which would strengthen God's people then—and in subsequent ages. The opening chapter sets the pattern and theme for the book; vivid imagery and symbolic language are used to capture a most striking and evocative vision of the risen, victorious Christ. No mention is made of the Satanic powers, the enemies of Christ's Church, who feature prominently in later chapters. Since the book is to show that Christ is the Victor, the Conqueror, who has the keys even of death and Hades (18), and that He remains victorious even when His Church seems to be defeated, it is highly appropriate that the opening chapter should be dominated by this vision of majesty and glory. Again and again throughout the book, glimpses of this vision are given (2.8; 5.9 ff.; 12.9 ff.; 14.1; 20.4; 22.3). Christ 'conquers death, Hades, the dragon, the beast, the false prophet, and the men who worship the beast. *He* is victorious; as a result, so are *we*, even when we seem to be hopelessly defeated' (Hendriksen). Difficult problems of interpretation in later chapters ought not in any way to obscure the central figure, the Risen Christ, whose word is 'Fear not, I am the first and the last'.

Questions and themes for study and discussion on Studies 39-44

1. What specifically Christian teaching may be illustrated from the account of Noah's Ark, and what is the O.T. justification for it?

2. What are the main similarities and differences between prophecy and apocalyptic, and how should each be understood?

3. What light do Mark 4.10–12 and Matt. 13.34 f. throw on our understanding of parables?

NINE

Obeying God's Word

45 : From Faith to Faith
1 Corinthians 2.1-16

In theory at least, it would be possible, though difficult, for a person who had neither driven nor even lifted the bonnet of a car to understand a technical book about the workings of the internal combustion engine. A person who attempts to understand a religious document without himself holding the religion set forth in it faces far greater difficulties. In theory, perhaps, it ought to be possible: in practice, adherents of a faith see it in a different perspective from that of outsiders. Christians have made some remarkably sensitive attempts to understand Islam, though a Muslim would find fault with even the best expositions. But when Paul talks about 'spiritual truths to those who possess the Spirit' (13) he is not talking of the differences between those who do something and others who merely study it, nor of the difference between 'insiders' and 'outsiders'. He is talking of entirely different kinds of people, those who are 'natural' (14) and those who are 'spiritual'. The verses clearly refer to regeneration. It is only those who have been 'born anew' by the direct action of God's Spirit who can understand spiritual truth (cf. John 14.26; Rom. 8.14–17). The reason for this is indicated in vs. 6–12. The Christian message is not a word of human wisdom. It has not been discovered through human enlightenment, like Buddhism, nor by 'logical' deduction, like humanism. It is the wisdom of God, disclosed to man by God Himself 'through the Spirit' (10).

All this does not mean that the human part of communicating Christian truth can be minimized. The balance between the human and the divine is indicated in vs. 1-5, verses which have too often been interpreted as justification for a presentation of the gospel which is intellectually weak or unrelated to the life of the hearers. What Paul disclaims is 'superiority' in 'words of wisdom'; he resists 'enticing' or 'persuasive' words (4). But he 'proclaims the testimony' (1), concentrating on Christ (2), and he presents a message (4). In Acts 18, his work at Corinth is described as 'arguing', 'persuading' (4), and 'testifying' (5). For eighteen months, he was 'teaching the word of God' (11). This was the human side of his ministry, which must have been exacting intellectually and physically, but all this was none the less human weakness. It was the 'demonstration of the Spirit' which was decisive. The word indicates 'rigorous proof'. The Spirit was convincing the hearers that the message was not merely historically accurate and intellectually satisfying, but divine truth—truth which was, and is, 'the saving power of God' (Rom. 1.16, NEB).

46 : Faith in God's Word

2 Kings 4.8–37

One of the simplest, most straightforward explanations of what faith means is contained in the account of Paul's shipwreck. To a group of terrified pagan sailors, who had long since given up hope, Paul says with amazing confidence, 'I have faith in God that it will be exactly as I have been told.' God had told him what would happen and he believed God. His confidence was not in the angelic messenger, nor in the words themselves, as though they had magic power. His trust was in God Himself, that He would do *exactly* what He had said.

The Shunammite woman is a vivid example of the same faith. She had not asked for a son, but obviously she longed for children; the news that she 'would embrace a son' was literally too good to believe (16). The birth of her son twelve months later was only a partial fulfilment of God's word, since the promise of a son meant an assurance that the line of her family would be continued. When the boy died of sunstroke a few years later (18–20), she did not 'accept' his death and go into mourning, as though God had changed His mind. Nor did she do nothing. She acted in faith. She told her husband, who only knew that the boy was off-colour, that 'it will be well' (23). She told Gehazi that 'All is well' (26, NEB). And then she put all the responsibility exactly where it belonged—on the man who had first given her God's promise, refusing to let him go until he had done something himself. Whether she expected Elisha to bring the boy back to life is not clear from the story, but it is clear that she expected something. Death was not the last word. The final word was with God. God never goes back on His promises. What He says He will do, He does.

For meditation : 'Never dig up in unbelief what you have sown in faith.'

47 : 'Today, when you hear . . .'

Hebrews 3.1–19

These studies began, in Heb. 1, with a question which many people ask; 'Why is God silent?' The answer of Heb. 1.1–4, that God has spoken and still speaks clearly and powerfully to our age through Jesus Christ, is emphasized again in 3.1. Jesus is the Apostle and High Priest of *our* confession. The phrase in Heb. 1.2, 'in these last days', which refers to the time between Christ's birth and His second coming, is crystallized into one word in Heb. 3, the significant word 'today' (7, 13, 15). The writer, knowing that Christ is the full and final word of God to man, and that in Christ God has said all that there is to say, puts a large, urgent question against every day—'Will today be a day when you hear God's word, believe it, and obey it?' Verses 18 and 19 make the connection between obedience and belief, or disobedience and unbelief, quite explicit. The two words are virtually interchangeable in the two verses.

The nub of the chapter is in vs. 12–15. The warnings are against 'an unbelieving heart' and 'the deceitfulness of sin', without any indication of which might come first. Presumably it may be either. On the positive side, we are to 'exhort one another' and to hold firm to that direct faith we first had. The word 'exhort' is the same as that which describes the Comforter in John 16. It can be used to describe the encouragements which two members of the same team might call to one another. The phrase 'we share in Christ' needs emphasis in a chapter which is rather sombre in tone. To share in Christ opens up endless possibilities. 'Christians . . . . . can always be expectant because they are living in God's "Today", and there is no knowing what may happen and there are no limits to His grace' (D. Webster). It is important to remember that the chapter is addressed to Christians. It is Christians who are urged to listen to God's voice, to believe, and to obey, and to do it now, today, every day, so long as 'today' lasts (13).

For meditation : 'I have been always looking to the future for opportunities to glorify Thee. I live in the future and not in this day that Thou hast given. A life of dedication I want to have, but I am longing to have it only in the future. I want to make my relations pure, only in the future. I am a Christian in a dream, living in an unreal future world, neglecting the marvellous opportunities Thou offerest me today. Lord, give me the strength to rise above the weakness of 'postponement' and continuously create in me a feeling of 'Life is Today', for tomorrow I may never be' (from Meditations of an Indian Christian).

'TODAY, when you hear His voice. . . .'